TY FOARD

EROS

PSALMS OF LOVE

Ty Foard

Eros

Psalms of Love

Eros
Psalms Of Love

Published by BLI Publishing, LLC
P.O. Box 1931
Cedar Hill, TX 75106
USA
469-557-1254 | www.BLIPublishing.com | info@blipublishing.
com

Book cover, layout and editing completed by BLI Publishing,
LLC. All rights reserved.

Published in the United States of America. Printed via
Createspace.

ISBN-13: 978-0692428696
ISBN-10: 0692428690

Dedications

Ty Foard

Taija…
You are the greatest story I ever told. My best-seller. No one can change the love I have for you.

Shirley…
I am because you are…love from the start.

The Twins…Sha and Char
I enough love to split between you two. You two inspire me to be a good example like a big brother should be.

Angela...
Baby girl. Love you sis.

Marcus...
Brother and friend. Proud of you.

Roosevelt and Tina Foard...
Your love saved me. I never will lose it.

Mary Bell, Rebecca, Jerome, Charles, and Gwen...
Thank you all from the bottom of my heart for all you did.

To all who have shared some form of love...
I love you back.

And To Her …
This dedication is yours before you are even mine.

TABLE OF CONTENT

Eros: Psalms of Love

PRELUDE: LOVELY INTRODUC- TIONS

In the middle of the day I received a text message from her. This was not uncommon. Since the very first night we shared a passionate kiss, she had randomly sent me daily text messages letting me know how much she was thinking of me. Sometimes they would be something simple as a generic emoticon smiley face blowing a kiss. She was creative with the emoticons, always finding one to match the topic of whatever conversation we were having. Other times she would send an encouraging phrase or a simple, 'Have a great day.'

This day for some reason when I felt the vibration from my Samsung Galaxy X phone I knew this was a different type of text. As I pulled the phone from its leather belt-clip case I could see her smiling face from the picture I had as her profile picture. It was my favorite of all of the selfies she had ever sent. Obviously, her beautiful caramel tone skin face was the center and focus of this masterpiece but one's eyes would easily get drawn into her slightly red laced pair of lips that always caught my attention. I have always had a thing for a nice pair of lips, if I deem them good I label them mentally as kissable. Not just a smack on the lips kind of kissable but kissable to where I want to suck on them like my favorite Jolly Rancher. Unlike other pictures though, this one was different to me because her dark eyes appeared so in focus that I could stare into them as if I was looking through the world's strongest telescope gazing into millions of light years of outer space. They make me pause every time I look at the picture.

Not to lose focus I quickly began to read her message. It read: 'Hello sweetie. I have a quick question that has been running through my mind all night...'

The message stopped just like that. Of course, it quickly bothered me. I really don't like when people send incomplete... wait the second part seems to have just come through.

The text continues: '...Sorry I accidentally hit the send button by mistake. I know you hate incomplete messages but here is the rest of the original message. What type of relationship do we have?'

I personally loved how she quickly got to the heart of her question without beating around the bush. Many times, women will state that they have a question and expect or wait for some type of response or approval to proceed. Then from my experience a lot of women will beat around the bush before asking what they really want to know.

I continued to read her message: 'I ask because I don't want to have any misunderstandings. I want to know the limit to my expectations when it comes to us.'

As I read her words a half smile comes over my face. I have met a lot of women over my life...lives. Very rarely has any woman that I have been involved with ever ask this simple yet complex question.

And this question is always a complex one to answer. So I carefully choose my words and reply without any long delay: 'What type of relationship do you feel we have and what type would you like to have sweetie?'

So maybe you notice that I was quick to reply, but not quick to answer the question. Sometimes we are quick to give a response without understanding the question. I have learned over the years that even though times change women rarely do. Most won't ask you directly what they want and if they do there is always more they want to know. Many times, they will ask you what I call set-up or bait questions long before you get to the root.

Seconds later I received her answer: 'I feel like we

have a great friend with benefits type of arrangement and I am happy with it if you are...'

I noticed this time there was no emoticon. I also notice that she ended her text with an ellipsis point. That's those three dots at the end of comments that represent an intentional omission of words, sentence. I knew that she was expecting either an agreement or a more optimist view. This next reply by me will be what could start a war or prevent one. I replied: 'That sounds great to me babe.' I ended it with two emoticons - one with the kissing face the other with the smiling tongue poking out.

Minutes later she sent a closing text message that read: 'I hope to see you tonight. I will leave the key in our spot...try not to scare me when you get in.'

Now this time she included the winking emoticon followed by three kissing ones. Amazing how even the most child-like things can now speak so much for adults.

"Hello sir."

This was the greeting I got from this beautiful young lady that was now standing in front of me. For a woman that stood maybe a good 5 feet 4 inches her well toned legs seemed to go on for days. She was wearing a nice fitted gray skirt that wrapped around her thin waist like it was a boa constrictor. Amazingly her rear-zip up blouse didn't have any room to be tucked in. Shocking to see her hair style of choice was conservative based on the other fashion statements she was making as its silky texture was simply pulled back into a ponytail. Although her hair was pulled back you could still see the brown wavy curls that flowed like a river in the Hill Country. The slight breeze seemed to toy with the few curly locks that seemed not to want to stay slicked down as they were meant to. Her dark hazel eyes created an eclipse with the brightly shinning sun that was attempting to glare off the side of her golden exotic skin completion. Her lips were not as full as I normally would prefer but she had a way of holding them out a bit that could convince you that size is overrated.

"I see you are not only on time for our lunch date, but you are early; most men of your caliber tend to be fashionably late," she said with the cutest grin on her face.

Her name was Amanda Starks. She was a thirty-one-year-old recently divorced attorney. We first met one night at a gas station. It was raining. I was just finishing up pumping my gas when she pulled up in her Audi Q7. Even with the rain coming down heavy I could see how pretty she was. I walked up and offered to pump her gas so that she would not get soaked. Not only did I pump the gas for her, but I paid for it. When I was done I jumped back into my car and drove off before she could get out and thank me. About a week later while at the same gas station she pulled up and asked, "Why did you just disappear that day sir?"

"I didn't disappear. I simply left when I was done," I replied.

"You must be one of those married men that don't wear his wedding ring in public?" she said to me as she stepped out of her candy apple red BMW that day.

"New car?" I asked.

"No, this is my other car."

"Nice," I said as I slowly walked around the car giving it a nice inspection.

"So, you are just going to ignore my question?"

I stopped my inspection to look her into her eyes, "Was that a question or was it just your prejudice observation?"

"Well I really don't know you…"

"For now, you don't…," I interrupted.

We stood there for about 20 minutes talking and it was like playing a long chess match. It seemed like we both were testing each other before we conceded and exchanged phone numbers. I tried to call her twice after that day, but she never answered the phone. I'm not much of a message leaver so I soon gave up on reaching her. Out of nowhere yesterday I received a text message from her inviting me to this lunch date today.

Sorry for the long sidebar and quick history recap. Sooo … where were we in this story. Oh yeah …

"I see you are not only on time for our lunch date, but you are early; most men of your caliber tend to be fashionably late," she said with the cutest grin on her face.

"I'm not what you can classify as the most men type," I replied as I stood up to greet her with a hand shake.

She quickly bypassed the hand and went for the full hug. As she hugged me she pressed her head up against my chest, checking the pecks, while taking one arm to the middle of my back assuring she controlled the length of the hug as her second hand somehow gently rubbed against the lower buttons of my fitted style Stone Rose shirt so that she could feel my abs.

As she completes her quick inspection she pulls away and says, "I can tell you are different because I sent you the invite and you never replied back saying you received it or that you were coming."

The look on her face gave off that she was impressed. We both gave each other that look like we knew where direction our conversation was quickly heading.

"So how did you know I would show?" I asked with a slight grin on my face.

"Because I just knew," she said as she pulled me

Ty Foard

closer to her as she tip-toed for a quick kiss on the lips. I pretended not to be moved in any way by the unexpected physically intimate gesture.

"How did you know I would really be here waiting on you?" she asked as she walked up to the table she had already reserved for us.

I pulled her chair back for her and said, "I didn't know…"

It would take me a thousand years to explain how this lunch date ended up in her downtown high-rise luxury apartment. Now before you attempt to judge me know that we never made it to her bedroom. I mean you are just getting to know me so don't be so quick to assume that I, like many men, can't control myself. I am not the type that can't prevent every good date from ending up with wet stained sheets, messed up hair do's after passionate lovemaking. Okay let's be honest, we just met so it would be more like sex with a little lovemaking. So let me assure you we did not mess up any bed sheets. Who needs a bed when you have a comfortable Maxdivani leather sofa? It was real and instant passion, what you may call natural chemistry. A chemistry that opened about three months of those same type of lunch

23

dates. She was so meticulous when it came to lovemaking. She knew what she wanted and how she wanted it. What she didn't know was, I was capable of anything physically she could imagine. Much to my amazement she was well equipped to give as much as she could take.

Everything was going well until one day she said she had fallen in love with me. That was the day I had to end it. It was against the code. The rules. The law. My job was to usher in love for others not myself. She quickly changed, but love can cause you to do some weird things. So, with a simple touch, I caused her to forget ever meeting me. She could bump into me in the streets and never recall we ever met, let alone had hundreds of hours of sex. And also, for the record, I promise you I never used any of my arrows on Ms. Amanda Starks or any other woman I may have been involved with.

Arrows? Yeah, I have those. Arrows that are invisible to the naked eye but more effective than any dating site or aphrodisiac. Nothing like a date drug, in my line of work I try to keep it on the straight and narrow. I never use my arrows whenever it comes to finding love for myself. When and if I will use them, it is to bring others together. I don't try to force people together who are not matches or who are not compatible. I let you humans make that mistake so in the end you can only blame yourself. You see these arrows have a way of causing you to experience the type of love that rarely dies. The love you hear in the melody of your favorite love song. The love writers try to explain in their deepest poem. I am making Valentine's Day every day.

No one is immune to the pierce of these love arrows, which brings us to my issue. Let me just say that I made the mistake of piercing myself by accident many years ago. To be exact 2,409 earth years ago. That day I found and fell in love with Syche. She is the most beautiful being I have ever seen. Even before the arrow I admired her beauty as did many of the men of her time. Over the many years I have tried to describe her beauty to others however as the days turn into years and the years turn into centuries like a broken jigsaw puzzle I lose the image of her in my head. Soon my purpose in this life became my curse. I broke the rules of the god counsel and even though my mother was one of the highest ranked goddesses she could not get me pardoned for my mistake.

You see no demi or full god was to ever love a human. So, I was to live my life in eternity inspiring others and guiding others to love yet not being able to fully receive love in return. As far as Syche, she was also punished, and her spirit was turned semi-immortal. This means every lifetime she only lives to the age of 33. Her body would die, and she would be reborn to new parents with no idea of this continuum. At each birth I would be able to identify her less and she would not know who I was if I happen to cross her path. Even though I have no idea how she looks, I have not forgotten the scent of her beauty and the smile on her face. I have vowed to outlast this punishment to find her. There have been at least 73 rebirths. I must find her, and I will, even though I have no idea how. So, for now all I do is travel from day to day helping others find, experience, and believe in love while deep down I search for my one true love.

No one is supposed to know who I am. So over time, in a million stories I am a myth, a legend. Some religions will start to label me and my kind as pagans or idols. It's funny that some people consider me a god while others call me an idol. I don't know what to call myself. I guess it depends on the person and their perception. I have no responsibility to mankind's religious or spiritual beliefs. We exist to help mankind, not to control or rule man. I have nothing to do with right or wrong, good or bad, evil or holiness. I have a power and I use it when I see the need. I have lived since man's creation. Though I appear and act like a man I am not what you would call a normal man. I have been called the god of Love, but I'm not love. Love is so much bigger than me. I work for love. I live for love. I exist for love. I am as much a slave to love as I am its symbol.

Though with my abilities my body ages at a rate much slower than any human. If compared to you I would have to have 400 human kind years to experience what you call one birthday. I can change my skin complexion, eye color, hair color, and my height to some degree.

I have decided that this year I was going to live in the open among "regular" men. My name is Eros.

Now before I go on any further please don't confuse me with that little child-like cherubim, Cupid. I have a lot of time on my hand so with some of that time I make sure that I keep my body in perfect shape. I am not vain but since I am making myself visible to the human eye I want to look appealing. I would love to walk around with my wings spread out, though they are things of beauty as they span about 15 feet, but there are some things the human eye and mind cannot handle. I have no race so over time I have spent time wearing many of the shades of Earth's eclectic skin colors and cultures. When I am around my kind I stand about 8 feet

8 inches, which is average height for the male beings. When I walk among humans I measure right at 6 feet tall.

I don't possess any special powers but I can make someone forget an experience with me. Many have figured out my identity over the years. I have a weakness for beautiful women and have on many occasions had my hand caught in the cookie jar, as you humans say. A few of these beautiful ladies have even seen me in my natural form, wings expanded and that intoxicating glow that rises from the skin. I never worry about them exposing me over the years simply because no one would believe them. The stories and confessions are entertaining, and they get more creative as the decades roll by. It adds to my myth, which adds to my purpose.

Humans desire love yet they only understand it based on their personal and selfish desires. I have the power to give them that desire. Throughout my life, I sometime am part of their desires and in other situations I arrange their moments. You can love me but if you seek me to love you the same way it would be a mistake on your part. I am everything you desire in a lover, yet I am not good for you personally. I will outlive you and out love you while still being committed to share that love to the world. If I was to give in completely then like many you would will mistakenly start to do more than just idolize me.

My mother was Love and Beauty, so I see her in all that is to be. My assumed father is War, the feared, the bringer of resolution to a conflict. My siblings are Panic, Fear, and Harmony and the youngest chases me. He is Anteros, dark and to balance me when it was thought I had no balance; for if I am seen as passionate or desired love he takes avenge for unrequited love. We are family and I miss them. My mother has commissioned me to return to the place we call home. Yet I can't return until I have what I lost. I seek that which has escaped me for many nights. I know she is somewhere on this earth, so this is where I will remain until I find her.

After being on earth for so long, I decided to live as a human, hoping that it would pass the time. I have a job. I purchased a home. I shop. I party. I attend sporting events, and I date. Yet I still manage to get lonely. When I first got here I spent a lot of my time indulging in the pleasure of women. Many women. When I say many it's an understatement.

You may be asking how am I able meet so many

women? Well it is because of my job. I am the radio show host of the nationally syndicated show Love Notes with Eros and Arrow. Five days a week, many women and some men call in to get love advice from me and my co-host, a beautiful young lady by the name of Arrow. Very interesting name, she has. Though it is her on-air name it is the same as her legal name just spelled without the "w". The industry and my fans love the fact that my name for all they know is Eros, but they also tag me as "Radio's God of Love", oh the irony in that title. So not only does this show allow me to "indirectly operate in my purpose of guiding lovers to a successful meeting," but it keeps me busy.

Somewhat.

The other thing this job does is it keeps me in somewhat of a spotlight. Women are always reaching out to me and at many times I entertain their advances. Now being who I am, I am violating the rules by living and enjoying this spotlight. A spotlight we "special" beings are supposed to stay out of. My mother is constantly sending one of my siblings to warn me of my renegade like behavior, but she knows that won't stop me. I'm having too much fun.

One day, we interviewed the alleged Doctor of Love,

Shan Morehouse on the show. Dr. Shan, her celebrity name, was a psychologist by profession and sex and relationship coach. She had a large social media following and was known to have many high-level celebrity clients. Trust me I was very eager to find out why she was crowned the expert on the field I was created to manage and from the look of things she was making a good living off it.

When she walked into the studio I was taken back because she did not look as I had expected. Standing about 5' 9" she had long athletic sculptured legs. I love nice legs, so I was instantly drawn to them. She either had a strong history in track and field or a religious like membership to 24hr Fitness. By the look on her face I could tell she knew they were best of show worthy because she dressed to assure any judge that they were winners. She was showing them off with a pair of Yves Saint Laurent lace-up designer shorts than gently hung off her small curvy hips. White shorts to be exact, which is my favorite color to see a woman wear. Those YSL shorts come with a $1,700 price tag, proof she doesn't mind paying for style. It was matched by designer t-shirt that carried the YSL brand. She wore a pair of turquoise and black high heels platform strap shoes. YSL grey clutch with matching silver choker, earrings, and watch combination to wrap up her accessories. I have an eye for fashion because I know women. I have known women for thousands of years. This was a woman that knew how to make herself standout in a good way.

Physically, Ms. Morehouse with her paper bag brown complexion had average size breasts and what I would rate as semi-full lips. Yeah, she was a guest and I was supposed to be working but I was looking. She wore Havana twists but only on the side of her head that wasn't shaved to a love fade. She kept a natural face with light make-up. Those lips were glossed over with a dark peach colored lip balm.

By the end of the show I had her questioning her own credentials. I taught her more about love in that thirty-minute interview than she learned in all her years of college. She started asking me so many questions that it appeared that I was the guest. Two hours after the show ended she and I were in the honeymoon suite at the Omni hotel. We didn't need a "honeymoon suite" but we took advantage of all the space.

She was open minded and creative when it came to the physical act of sex. Her flaws were minor. As much as I enjoyed our time together, I could not get the organic connection to her heart. I felt no fire in her soul. For a woman, having a man that is unable to awaken the sensual side of her soul will never be complete. Physically, I could be everything she ever fantasized. With a simple touch of my fingertips on the right parts of her body I could cause her to climax. Every time my lips would touch any part of her she would release. As I interpret her moan infused talk back, this was the first time she has had more than one orgasm in one sitting. After this day she would tell her girlfriend of how she lost count after number nine, and of course they will not believe her because I will be long gone leaving no trace that I ever existed. I am a god, history and myths call me the God of Love, so I should not have no problem sensing love in the depths of a human's soul or heart.

Anyways she was highly talented with how to use her body. Mentally, she had given up on intimacy and real love. Her walls were so strong that I could touch them almost as easy as the walls of the buildings outside. Spiritually she was not connected to the rest of the world. Lost and hurt by past loves, so much so that she suppresses her feelings.

So as usual I had to decide if I would hang around and see where this lead us or move on to the next. At least if I stay the sex will be earth shaking. It always does. If you ever felt a tremor, then you get what I am referencing to.

Maybe one day I will be able to tell you more of my story. As for now I have a few passages, poetry, and thoughts to share with you. Many humans and beings are inspired by the journey through love's universe. Some are of the erotic descriptions I saw while in the dreamlands of love. And some are the things many of us want for. I wrote many of them longing for her. Her? She knows who she is. I must find her for myself.

I call them Psalms of Love.

Wings spread.

I am Eros.

Take flight.

PSALMS OF LOVE

Wings Spread: Eros Speaks

If You Don't Mind

If you don't mind...
I would like to get so close to your lips
that no one can tell yours from mine...
so close that you start to speak every word
that forms in my mind
until we dance to the rhythm of verbal echoes
and get high off the sweet breath that is blown...
and like tasting sweet candies
I taste the most intimate regions of your soul...
for the rest of my days will I hunger for you...
So, this gets mixed with tongue tricks and
metaphoric positions combined with slow humming licks...
The angels envy our tunes
less they fall...
So, they spread wings and you speak to my lips
from your lips to get closer...
closer

Crush

How did I fly this far only to fall in love…?
So now I have the similarities of a fallen angel
Fear me not for I bring you good tidings of great joy…
You can't see me
you only feel me…and I can't touch you
Forbidden … how hard is it for the darkness to exist in the light
I have been wrestling with angels in thought all night…
And I vowed not to let go until they bless me
To speak to you…
Just for a moment…for in your world I don't exist…
How hard is it for the light to allow the darkness to stay?
when it enters the room…
the creator is calling me back for my next assignment
he knows my heart, so he keeps me moving …
but somehow in the middle of this heavenly rush
I saw you, and developed a crush

Dear Diary

(I thought of her today)
I wish that she would know every moment
I think of her.
Every moment I fight to forget her…
But much like the wind
Invisible to my eyes
You…are always there…
Unable to feel me as I feel you
Unable to hear me as I you
So, I continue to write you daily as if
Love is a fantasy
In the pages of this silent diary…
Dear Diary… (I thought of her today.)

Dear Diary: Day 5

A man finds someone to love
Someone who is willing to give him all
He never has found a way
To let go of a first love
The first love
A love that was more a dream than reality
A dream he wants to dream
Over and over again
And if the love in the dream is to fail
Why has this cupid toyed with me?
The day our paths crossed
Did he not shoot his arrow?
An arrow not meant to pierce my heart
An arrow traveling to find your love
Why did destiny push me in its path?
If my words are really just the result of my fear
Then you too
Dream as I dream…
This is day is 5
(I thought of her today…and I smiled)

I Pray

I can hear you sing to me
So sweet it is
The honey bees deem it
The sweetest melody
One that you
Wrote especially for me
Though I sit alone in a house
That appears to be empty
I hear your footsteps approaching
The doors of my heart
...I pray that I am everything
You ask for...
I pray in this empty vessel
You find favor to pour...
Your grace...
To fill that missing source of joy...
Can I be granted to see with eyes and mind?
the things that make you smile
Can I be given the reason to smile?
And carry you over life's hardest miles...
Am I ...Can I ...will I be

But the only sin committed
Was the moment I tried to stop, loving you
Surely goodness and mercy will follow you

Lil Time

I just want a moment of your time
I promise to be gentle as I make all
Of my attempts to poetically get into your mind
It's like…
Wet and cool going down your throat…
That branded style of poetic wine I quote
Feasting on your grace
So tasty I'm always ready to dine
Have you spread across my words?
And in between the blue lines
Please forgive my metaphors
I promise to take my time
You see they say time waits for no man
But for you woman
I promise to do all I can
Placing you on my center stage
And holding you like a jazz singer holding his mic stand
A sax player holding that sweet horn
Giving us good sax…loving you
With both lips and both hands
Speaking words into the valley of your peace…

We call them wetlands
A lil naught thought of
Bed sheets gripped tight with sweaty hands
So, for a lil time…let's get naughty

Joy Ride

So, if I promise to take
On a wild ride
Will you forget how fast time flies
And before that moment comes
Can you look into depths of my eyes?
And moan in a key of monotone
How we can both take our time
And make the shakes
They will stop right
Before the time of forever
So, if we leave
We leave, we leave together
So, when we come
We come
And like fun we come together
Don't move
Please don't stop this groove
Don't move
We at least not until we are
Done with due time during do time
I promise to take my time …as we take this joy ride.

Let's Do This

Can we do this…
Love each other
Hold each other
Sweet love like natural honey
Or rich and oily like the purest butter
And all the recipe calls for now
Is for us is to be with each other
So, come…let's do this
Let's take each other to the max
Releasing a love
Like sweet lyrics on nice mellow tracks
Sipping on each other like wine
Moaning and groaning to sexy rhymes
Knowing each other's wants
Reading between the lines…
The keeper of the sheets
Busy like the rush hour streets
So, let's get lost in this love
And when we are found
We do it repeatedly
You have me writing to be in
With you
Doing the things, we do

Love Testament

I was once lost
But now as I stare at your smile
I am twice found
You are the tone that gives richness to
My poetic sounds…
Amazing…
Once blind
But through your eyes
Twice I see…
My life has been tossed to
And forth
Like a ship in the middle of life's raging sea
The waters that once drowned me
You took and baptized me
I am born again
As together we take each other's hand
I am bragging to the angels of how
I love your Love
…woman
The day you came to me
Rib of me

Ty Foard

Now love of me
Wrapped me in a robe of peace
For my taste of the forbidden
Had left me naked to now see
But you opened my path to
Gracefully cover me…
The way you touch my body
Will be written as a testimony
One that can be sung with love sentiment
But I will record it
Not old or new
For it will be scribed the
Love Testament
I will be your disciple
12 times we will quote this love epistle
Much more than sexy and poetic
Rhetoric…this will be so eclectic
So, let he that has ears hear,
My body reaches the ultimate
Release when you are near
You gave me the true

Mange a tois
Loving me physically, mentally and spiritually
How one forms a trinity
Now we find ourselves trapped up in a
Poetic matrimony
Heaven is wherever you are
So, when you step into paradise
This day…Remember Me

She Flows For Me

She flows from me, like water so cool she calms me.
On dark filled roomed nights she goes straight through me.
She moves with style, with flavor, with grace.
In many ways for many days for always I will love her in the
unconditional ways.
Listen to the way her hips start to sway as the next coming of
Nina Simone plays…
we take turns transforming these new cats back into the real
cats
from back in the good old days…
Yes, I will always love her.
I want to make love to her and long to make love because of
her,
only for her,
I can't wait to be in her presence, her space.
I want to die consuming her scent and watching her lyrically
made up face.
Like sweet lips on the opening nights of open mics
a kiss from the prose she flows causes my mind, my body,
my soul to ignite.
On fire, she is the one that I desire

Eros: Psalms of Love

as I take time out of the dog summer days to write haikus to her…
for her I'll do anything…
like have mass choirs sing about the joy she brings…
she is my lady and she will never sing the blues…
because her heart I never want to lose…
so never will I allow cupids arrow for her to pass me…
so jazzy together we walk in John Coltran shoes…
hard starched jeans much more than Billie we play her holiday blues…
magnolia flowers in her hair…I can't help but stare…
she will be the sonnet that I will create…
So, if I am the captain of my own fate
then now I take ship and sail for her on the seven seas…
and pray for the calmness of the seas on bended knees…
see Anthony may sing calm songs of come home to his Charleen
but as for me…
never known to be greedy… all I need is my Lady…
and to this flow I will call her my Poetry.
she flows for me...she'll always be my baby...
she flows
ttf2018

Ty Foard

Love's Truth

I hear love and passion truth's...
When I see your actions...
I see passion when I feel, touch, and taste your words...
I take breaks often and snack on your images in pieces
broken up like fractions…
I am your math wizard and I add peace and happiness to your
life…
And take away pain and hurt with RoyalTy moves…but you
can call them subtraction…
Understanding there no rhyme or reason...
For you to ever be leaving...
You shall always be...right here...
Damn what the critics and calendars say…you shall be right
here…
Sweet lady You are not a season...
You are my YEAR...
So Let me speak this into your inner ear and make it
Crystal clear...
You will be the rest of my years...
Like mad poets...
We will give birth to generations on the Center Stage...

Make love on every turn of the page...
As you become one with me and my love
And we form the holy trinity...
As I lay you across the earth that I have created and
Open up the gates of your heaven...
And hearken to your angels as they say come...come into
me...
Come with me into thee…
See into me…
Taste intimacy …which is into-me-see…
And though I may not have been good for the ladies of my
past…
It was you I was created for so no one else's attempt could
have last…

Heaven...Must Be Like this

I believe that Heaven must be like this...
words that come to mind when you slide your finger slightly
up my spine...
as the angels spread their golden wings across the seven
clouds and the host of arch's open with soul stirring love
songs ...and the saints rise as they begin to sing...
with sweet notes and spiritual like quotes springing off of
Gabriel's harp as we make love through paradise...your grace
can save me...your passion flows for me to the beating of my
heart...stop the troop spread your sweet wings and fly with
me...
let's cross out rugged death come rise with me...
for it was after three days your love saved me ...
so place your hand into my hand and lets pave these streets
gold and build many mansions to store the revelations of
what peace and harmony really looks like...surround them
with twelve pearly gates to keep all the hell out and live in
this blessing for an eternity...you are the substance of my
faith and seeing you is the evidence of all that I've hoped

for...so the holy scripts will be my new testament and I will forever learn from the old so that when you come to receive the salvation of this union you will be able to say with great, completion of peace of mind in a state of pure bliss...I believe that Heaven must be like this...

3.

It is believed that God created man so he would have someone with free will to fellowship with. A desire said so that this free willed being could experience the fullness of his creators love.

Naturally because such being was created this way, it would also seek love in order the same fullness of love…

A religious writer once penned a verse… "…though I have the gift of prophecy and understanding all mysteries, all knowledge, and though I have a faith so that I can move mountain…if I have not love…then I am nothing

Even if we ignore the signs in our lives…there will always be an inner need, desire, and thirst for love.

So this day I was asked
what do I want for?

A question that has an answer that is quite simple. I want for you to allow me to love you with that is within me I want for you to love me just the same…

Writing For Her

I used to write about her before I ever met her…She was the inline and the outline of every love letter and love poem that I ever wrote. I always knew it was love. It was real love, true love. I wrote for her, I wrote to her, and I wrote about her for many years…

She was much more to me than a dream. To say she was a fantasy would merely be an understatement. If I could see her face or tell describe her body from head to toe…my description would be spoken in an unknown tongue…

All I know is that she was out there and one day I would find her…She would get a chance to read the things I wrote and know that I have waited and written all of my life to see her, to hold her, to place my lips onto hers…

Writing for her…

Ty Foard

Gold

With eyes of gold, with hair of gold
Behold this very soul
My soul sister…neo-bold sister
Sweet ebony bronzed skinned baked by the sun…
Please, for I will
Cherish her like pure
Gold…

Your Touch

...you touched me
Without lifting a finger
Your smile burned my heart
Without a single flame of fire
It was your words
That gave birth to me
As they took journeys off of your lips
Cutting cords that connected me to loneliness
You are the woman in my dreams
Before I lay down to sleep
You amaze me
Cause you found a way to hold me
Without touching me
So I pray for that touch
And thank God for your touch…

Silence

...he told me of how
He lost his words
When he looked into your eyes...
Please gently touch my face
Then feel the wind blow
Smell the rose in my hand
See the love in my eyes
Taste the sweet savor of the mood
Being close to each other produces
...yes I lost my words the day I looked into your eyes
Every noun and verb went to one of my five senses
No sentence I can created will be absent of you
Rub my lips
To hear my feelings
As they tell you of my love...

Pray With Me

Let us pray that
We become all that God would have
Us to be
Let us pray that
We understand all that our Lord wants us to be
Let us pray that we stay in his Will and give birth to this life
Prepared for us, me as your husband, you as my wife
I shall never worry about losing you
…cause God sent you
So when I pray, I pray for our growth
In his will
So I ask you to pray with me still…

... For You

God invited me into his arena of love
Where he showed me showered me with his love
Where my love for him could grow
Where I learned to love
Where I began to truly understand love
…it is there that I met you
…it is there that I felt your grace
…it was there where I wanted to stay…
Can you…
Will you…
…when God invited me in
He gave me two tickets…
So I have one ticket for me and one for you…

I Could Do

You ask what could I do?
I know I cannot live without you
You are in my mind
You are in my dreams
Thinking of what I could do
All I know is I
Cannot let you go

Tell Me

If there was a chance for us to be together forever
…would you tell me
Or would you allow me to remain a prisoner in my own
mental fantasy…
Soaring through the skies
Your smile is the wind that's beneath me
My wings only flap to the song your voice
Sings as if they were controlled by some love sick spell
Like an angel I await to blow
Heaven's trumpet at your arrival
I'll be your poetic arch-angel …surname me Gabriel…
Can you tell when you look at me
I am born again
I prayed that you were formed from this rib
Out of the side of me…flesh of me…bone of me
So that you could call me your first man
Like I was to be named Adam
Meeting you on the eve of the day
Like the forbidden fruit
You belong to another
Which leaves this fantasy asunder

History misspoke when it noted Zeus god of thunder…
Until I pulled down bad dreams with the hammer of the folk
lore of Thor…
I have lost you…searching for you through the sky like a
falcon I soar…
And the thoughts of you imprisons me
My cell is covered by the thoughts of you and they cover me
in my solitary…
For I have been sentence to long for your souls kiss for
eternity
I lock the doors myself for there is shame in my sin…
I have created true love yet wrote it off as a true fantasy
And now with no warden I have cast away the key…
So though this shall forever haunt me…
If there was a chance for us to be forever…
I would pray that it is together…
Would you tell me…
Would you…

The Gift

Open this box
A gift from me to you
It may be small but the meaning and
Thoughts are large and true
…please be gentle with my gift
for it is fragile if not handled with care
I have taken much time and have worked so hard
to prepare this gift I give to you
I'm sure you will enjoy it for
I cherish it…
I find you very special
and appreciate your love
…that is why
I am giving you
This gift
…my heart

Tonight

Bubble baths…
Chocolate cherries…
Fine wine…
Sweet cream dipped strawberries…
Candlelight…
Moonlight…
A cool breeze…
A midnight tease…
Whip cream…
Body steam…
Warming lotions…
Not too fast but not slow motion…
Marvin Gaye…
Getting it on to the games we play…
Luther songs
…how can lace ever be wrong…

Tonight all of these things would be nice…
Maybe they would give us so
Much more to do
But tonight all I really want

Ty Foard

Is you…
Tonight…

Excited

You have come
Back into my life…
Do you know how I feel…?

Ty Foard

Syn. Of Love

God…
Or an attachment, passion, a yearning
Rapture, emotion, sentiment, cherishing, devotedness…
…my feeling for you

One Day

One day I dreamed of love…
One that would wrap me with the substance of happiness
One that would show through a timeless
Picture of us…
One that would seem too crazy to be true
One that says you were made for me
And I was made for you…
One that would make me stand here today
Before the world and look you in the face and whisper I love
you
While the minister is yet still speaking
Words that make what I have felt for you
For all this time now official
But it's funny and beautiful at the same time
Cause this is just a ceremony
Be we have already vowed to change the law
That says one plus one equals two
Because you and I will always equal one…
So one day I dreamed of this love…
And one day I found this love…
And one day we are saying I do…

But this love that you share with me…
Is for
One
And I want this love…for one life
So remember until death do us part
I will love only
One…

Adam's Evening

…Awaken from a deep sleep.
…that which was within me is now before me.
…and in the mist of this garden
I am relived…
For as the sun sets before my eyes stands my Eve
…stay wrapped in the essence of beauty from with…
…and if this day was never to come
Maybe longing for one like you too much would have been
the first sin.
…like before there was a Fall of Eden
God saw fit to co-habitat this garden
Bone of my bone and flesh of my flesh
…we shall give birth to all the generations of many nations.
…less we overcome the tree in the mist.
…for it has been placed before us as a test.
…to hold you is matrimony and
To make love to you
Shall be called holy…
As heaven and earth move to the songs of our love
And our actions will be recorded by the angels up above

...so before any genesis I write...
Let me press my lips against your lips
For they will be known as the keys to paradise
...be my wife
My wo-man...as I am your
A-dam
...and it has been revealed that your are
My Eve...

The Wind...I love how the wind feels when it brushes across my face on a warm day. I often from whence it came...because it brings a cooling...Have you ever had someone that made you think of them whenever they were away. I often that the wind allows me to feel them.

The Wind

I love to feel
The wind blow
I often imagine
From whence it has come...
Has it touched your lips?
Has it cooled your body?
Has it tickled your nose?
Has it whispered in your ear?
How I wish like the wind I could...
I love to feel the wind blow...

Whispering Winds

Listen for my whisper in the winds
Whenever you hear a voice calling your name
If you should ever see a rose in full bloom
When a raindrop touches your hand
if a love song touches your soul
When it seems you have no friends
Listen for my whispers
Cause my love travels through the wind
Have you ever heard whispering winds?

Forgiveness

Forgive me…
I wonder if the wind blew hard enough
Could it carry me away?
Is the sea deep enough to drown my love?
The love which shines like a light in a dark world with eyes
close…
Even in a deep sleep it still leads me to you…
When the sweetest melody stops playing
I will continue to dance to your heart's beat
Is the sun hot enough to burn your love out of me?
Forgive me
I can't stop loving you…

By Any Chance

Excuse me
But if I may have a moment of your time
…someone said you were
Searching for love…
By any chance
Did you notice the day I,
Passed your way?

A Problem Solved

Some say
It is so hard to find true love
Tell them
To try opening up their
Heart's eyes

Stop Running

Have you ever ran?
…what about from love…
Give up cause
I'm going to always be here…

Ty Foard

Pain...Have you ever long for a past love...some believe love hurts...but actually losing love is what causes pain. Realizing that maybe what we thought was love was not is one of the most severe pains you can go through emotionally.

Hold

Close your eyes
I need you to feel this hug
That I am giving you right now
And even though you are hundreds of miles away
I am saving this one just for you
And I hope it allows you to release your pain
And if tears need to fall
Then let them fall for I have come prepared to catch them all
Let us build bridges over the waters of your pain
I want to hold you until you crossover to a land
Of peace…
Allow me to hold you…

Tears That Don't Fall

Who can wipe the tears that never fall?
Who can answer my cry?
…when they can't hear my call?
My tears burn like rays of the midday sun
Sometimes the pain
Forces me to scream how I am done…
But then who will hear
The words that I say
Why is it that life has done?
me this way…
Give me… Truth
I spoke to the wind
When my soul cried
Keeping my tears inside
I worked hard… my pain I tried my best to hide
I spoke to the silence
Around me and asked them…who?
She answered…
She said
I will be there for you
Then I was given three wishes

And a promise that they would come true
The funny thing is that
I used my three wishes on you…
Now I take away
Nothing but I gain more heartache and more tears…
So, who will wipe the tears that now fall
You wiped the first ones away
But why?
Was it so I would have more room for the tears that were
produced
The day you walked away from me
I'm sure your reply would be the classic words…
I'm very sorry
…we will always be friends
Sure, after I return to life

Truth

I spoke to the wind
When my soul cried
Keeping my tears inside
I worked hard… my pain I tried my best to hide
I spoke to the silence
Around me and asked them…who?
She answered…
She said
I will be there for you
Then I was given three wishes
And a promise that they would come true
The funny thing is that
I used my three wishes on you…
Now I take away
Nothing but I gain more heartache and more tears…
So, who will wipe the tears that now fall
You wiped the first ones away
But why?
Was it so I would have more room for the tears that were
produced
The day you walked away from me

I'm sure your reply would be the classic words…
I'm very sorry
…we will always be friends
Sure, after I return to life

Silence

...he told me of how
He lost his words
When he looked into your eyes...
Please gently touch my face
Then feel the wind blow
Smell the rose in my hand
See the love in my eyes
Taste the sweet savor of the mood
Being close to each other produces
...yes I lost my words the day I looked into your eyes
Every noun and verb went to one of my five senses
No sentence I can created will be absent of you
Rub my lips
To hear my feelings
As they tell you of my love...

Ty Foard

Special Dreams

I lay here in my bed with tears
rolling down my face
…my sleep was interrupted by a strange noise
…my dreams ended at the start of this new reality
In my sleep I dream and in my dream
I had you in my life…
Dreams can be so special…

Where Are You?

I see you
…even though you are not even here
I feel the softness of your skin
…even though you are not near
I hear your voice
As it tickles my ears
and your words are so clear
yet I understand them not
the same words that I watch slide off your lips a lot
…I still understand them not
…and when I ask
You run
Yet I am the one lost
because you are so clear and so near to me
…yet so far away which cause me
to live in a state called confusion
my heart screams to reach a logical conclusion…
how can I touch you when you are
really not here
how can my eyes focus on you
when you are nowhere near

Ty Foard

how can I love you
even though you are long gone
…and even though you did not call
I am answering my phone
I still remember feeling you in my arms
Yet my heart is the one that longs for the touch
My words are in chaos but
Simplified just means
I love you…yet for some reason
You only exists in my mind
But it is you in the physical that I seek to find
And I know you are there
Cause my soul feels you…but I don't know from where
where…

Always I Have

I love you now…just as I always have
I have been traveling
Around this world of love have
…sometimes I sit in caves of loneliness
and times come that put my heart to the test
wondering if another could ever take your place
but in my book of happiness
there has always been a picture of your beautiful face
the sweet melody of the newest love songs
come to sooth my mind
but deep in my heart I know
that another's love I will never find
cause at the end of every one of my rainbows
are memories of you…
and they tickle my belly with the funny
things we would do together
and the smart things you would say
…now whenever the wind takes time to brush against my
face
My mind wonders deep into the outers of space

…so sometimes I wish I was a star
So I could see everywhere you are
…like freshness of love and grace
I wish I was the summer rain
So that I could rain across your face
I remember what we use to have
And I love you now just as I always have

Gone

...here I sit
Wishing all of my feelings were gone
Denying that our time together was wrong
...back then I would sit around and long...
...for the day...I would sit around
and long for the day I would be strong
when my heart could beat without pumping for your heat
I picked a rose for you
And burned a candle for you
I wrote a poem for you
And penned a song also with words to are so true
The rose has never died
And the candle is still alive
My poem is often recited on the air waves of the v-vibe
And the song is played daily...sound system pumping
through as we ride...
I tried to turn the page
I tried to come of age
But my tears began to roll into rivers that flow into peaceful
brooks

Again I tried to turn the page only to find I was really at the
end of this book
So my heart beats for you
My soul exists for you
My love somehow scared you
You could not believe it was so true
Tried to stay strong
Yet you said our time together was wrong
Back then I would sit around and long for you
Cause even though you were there you still was gone…
Just like now you are gone
I sit around
This world has no clue
What true love can do…
Am I the last that believes?
Love is always true
I believed in you
I trusted in you
I lived just for you
…yet now I have to gain a new foundation to get strong

But as I turn the page I realize that you are now gone
Now I sit around and long…
Cause in my heart my
Love for you has not gone…

May I...

So lovely
So precious
…so why does the wrong person
Always touch your heart…leaving you alone
And all you really want…
for is someone to give
Their heart sincerely…

Pray With Me

Let us pray that
We be all that God would have
Us to be
Let us pray that
We understand all that
Our Lord wants us to be
Let us pray that
We stay in His Will
And give birth to this life that's prepared for us,
Me your husband,
You my wife.
I never worry about losing you
Cause I know who sent you
So when I pray I pray for our growth
In God's Will
So that is why I ask that you pray with me still

Ty Foard

Fallen For

It was that day
My eyes were truly opened
For so long, so blind
Then your word, they came
And blinded eyes were now opened
Opened to see a world
Thought to only exist
In one's dream
Opened to see a woman
Who was more than
The woman of one's dream
Forgive me now
If I should stumble
For with these new eyes
One…at times may fall
Forgive me now
If another owns your heart
For it is this same one
Who for your heart
Has fallen for

Fly Away

Are you an angel…
For if so please do go
Are you an angel…
For I have got to know
Where has thy hidden
Your wing to fly
Are they so glamorous
They are hidden from my naked eye…
So, what is your reason
To follow me around
Where is that
Beautiful heavenly gown
Like the love of yester-times
You have come my way
Are you an angel…
(for just like her)
You just may fly away

Can You...

Can you give up what you love?
…to save the one you love…
Cause real love
Is always giving
And has no real concern about losing
Do we think about what it is
We are choosing
Neglecting what we're really losing
Can love be described as give and take
But what if in giving
You give up
And in take
You take away for love's sake,

Letting Go

Would you mind if I let you go?
On a warm night I wondered
If I let you go
Would my life still have a peaceful flow?
Or would I be a simple man
Always moving, always on the go
Would the robin bird sing a new song?
And would my shadow get smaller
As the days went on
Could I reach out and touch
Another's heart as I once did to you
Could I still write all these nice rhymes?
And call her honey boo
You know I bet I could
But I never would
Attempt to call another my
One baby and it be true
Cause somehow none of it would be true
Cause I know I would never
Risk letting go of you…

Yesterday

I find myself thinking
Of you
Sitting around remembering you
I think about the songs
That would play when we would sit and hold hands
Know now, I just sit
Looking at my lonely hands
I feel like the moon
With the stars so far away
My mind won't let go of yesterday
To just be able to jump
Back to another day
But life is not fair
I can't get my way
Like a leaf in the middle
Of the ocean
My heart is empty...so it moves
Without any motion
I can't help to think
Of the past
Now I realize good times always

Don't last…
I wish I could jump
Back to another day
But my mind won't let go of
Yesterday…

Ty Foard

True Dreams

In my dreams you kissed
…another's lips
In my dreams you touched
…another's heart
In my dreams our love
…was not so good
In my dreams you left me
…as my tears came
Why do some say that Dreams don't always come true…
I sit here wishing
…it was true…

By Any Chance

Excuse me,
But if I may have a moment of your time…
Someone said you were searching for love…
By any chance
Did you notice
The day I passed your way?

A Problem Solved

Some say,
That it is so hard to find,
true love…
tell them
to just open up
their heart's eyes

Do You Know

Do you really know
What you did to me?
You opened my eyes,
And now I can see…
Do you really know
How you touched me?
Something I only thought
Could happen in my fantasy?
You made the winds in my
Life come to a gentle calm-
Your smile gave me a
Tingle in the center of my palm-
All of a sudden I,
Vowed that I could stand the falling rain
Your eyes promised to love me
And to ease all my pain
You have to understand that when…
…you hurt, I do too-
And you don't mind taking charge
When I have no clue…
Do you really know

What you did to me
caused me to climax with every word you did speak...
adding new life to my heart with the life of your sweet scent
my breath was gone and I
had no clue of where it went
but I have no problem
with having to breath like this...
do you know...I always await your kiss...
do you know...you make me feel this
love thing?

TO MY MORNING BIRDS:

The Petal...

...yesterday a petal fell from my rose...
like a leaf from the tree out back of my grandma's
wind the winds of life strongly blows...
...she was a beauty among many...
part of a beautiful flower but I valued her individuality...
as we travel down life's tracks
we should always remember
that we can never take a step back
a fallen tear can never roll back
so I hold this petal in my hand remembering the smiles and
the good times
like part of life...wanting but knowing I can never put it
back...
prepare your heart and soul...each day everything grow old
and we never know how tomorrow will unfold...
so even with sadness I will find happiness for the time I was
allowed to receive the beauty that this petal gave us...
and all of the scents of love she gave us...
fighting to the end to make this rose of life beautiful for those
of us that took the time to notice...
yesterday a petal fell from my rose...

...in the memory of a beautiful warrior and beautiful supporter Kimberly Foulks...will miss you my dear Morning Bird
...in memory of a friend who would come and listen to my poetry. Kim Foulks

Art Form

If I was a painter
I would spread your image across the canvas of a thousand
Spoken word stages
And brush your eyes across all of my journal's pages
I want to display you for you are my art form...and you have
release all my artistry from its locked cages...
You are my art form more than just in words that leak off 11
by 8, blue-lined pages
Your walk gives me the rhythm used to conduct
A new love symphony
Every instrument in tune
Blowing with full kissable lips in perfect harmony
...like rain drops on my soul...you shower me...and I rejoice
for you have found a way to entertain me...
your hips give shape to the dance moves of our second act
and it takes place to the count of three steps from our
bedroom...
and by everyone, two step we fully will be consumed...
until we are ready to burst like new flowers ready to bloom...
so mental and yet so sensual
in our minds we find each other's favorite tune...

like fire when I get close to you I get warm…when I made
the bet on love
you where the prize and lucky charm, my art form
now lay me down to sleep on nights like this our actions
write exotic sonnets
like spreading across the living room floor until we are feast
on each other
on the dining room table…
the sweet savor of art juices, flavor like cherry, strawberry…
if we are able
to open totally…I desire your sweetest peach…
as I finger paint across your body until I hang over your
deepest valley
for I don't mind reaching…
wet paint…signed …no harm…for you will be my art form

Now Offers Me Completion...

And I sit here enjoying your touch's sweet sensation…you have enter my heart with your love's mental penetration… and now you are the subject to my poetic dictation…the ink in my pen flows as you are my inspiration… and I have question myself is this lust, an urge, a fantasy, or some cheap fixation…a feeling that I thought only existed in the halls of my imagination…like fine wine over my lips…I cherish your sweet savor…and I understand that… the power of your honesty and character is my favorite flavor…you are my lady more than just in words…for others wonder about the business of our bedroom…them believing this thing between us is just physical…or so they assume…but what they don't know is we have the power to cause each other to climax to an unheard levels of soul stirring joy, happiness, and admiration just by walking into the same direction…or entering from different doors in a crowded room…and with a simple glance at each other our life filled four play sessions looms…a love unspoken has become the result of the 6 days of our creation…and what was once just a shapeless void has found salvation…the beginning is our offering and the power of spoken words is our sacrifice…with physical and spiritual dedications…and this eternal love is our resurrection…so take rest as I Am shall make you the spiritual source of my Sabbath… you are my covenant…and I shall not have no other lover before, after, or during thee…be baptize in the waters of love with me…my missing rib has to be in thee… so if I be Adam please never Eve me…give birth to a blessed family…and in your heart and I shall find shelter… your are my weather…to rain away the dryness of pain…to snow and freeze…the frustration of others who once presented false love…and to shine the rays of your sun to cause a smile to bloom from my heart and soul…your wind will cause me to never grow old…forever young…as I roll in a bed of fresh grass…escaping the bugs… only to awake and see that I am wrapped in your hug…I will protect you forever my true love…so if father time and mother nature ever try to take you away they will feel my wrath…me plus you equals so must just listen as our hearts and souls beat out the math.. all my life I have had the question… but no formula have ever give me resolution…you…now are my solution…and in you I find completion…you have found a way to touch me…and I know your soul told you how…so understand me when I look at you and say with so much love…now offers me completion…

Saved

Salvation,
You are the love of my life
Take me and hold me close
Baptize me in your kisses
Take me to the water
And submerge me
Under the sea
Your kiss is my lock and key...
Prisoned by a love that will out live
The shores of eternity
You are my lily
Both deep in the valley and laying
Right next to me...
Oil me ...
For I am anointed
You love me like no other
So daily I will come with tear to wash your feet
And in the middle of the night I will thank the
God I am created after
Cause, you have figured out how to love me...
There was no mystery

Ty Foard

You just loved me right

Solar Peace

The stars are ours so let's make our bed on Mars as Saturn
rings become our dance floor & Jupiter, Uranus, & Neptune
is ours to explore with Pluto in the back and Mercury our
front door...tell Venus she can't stay, cause she only gets
in the way...so maybe it's good for us to skip work and be
together both night and day...as I grab hold of this hot comet
watching the way your sweet hips sway...is this more than
just a study of the heavenly bodies
Or a full mix of nice similes'...as my creativity orbits the
possibilities of bringing your fantasies into many realities...
and giving you more than just outer space...I give you peace

Awaken

Now that the chains of loneliness have been broken…
my eyes are open, and I have been awakened…
awaken from this deep sleep,
missing a rib from my side
nature tells me that you shall be my bride…
being that which I have been loving through heavenly
wishing
Dear Eve, to love you…
I have been awakened…
to love you I have been commissioned…

The Pretender

So maybe I'm the great pretender
On blank pads I lay down the lines of my love and through a
single mic
On a center stage I send it to her
Pretending that it is for the audiences that sit before me
Pretending that I am gifted with the gift of gab and free verse
I drink of the artistic waters of love
Leaving my tongue wet yet when the lights go out
The chambers of my heart beat with thirst…
So they cheer for me and I welcome their Applause
But my only true desire my only true clause
Is for her know that I am lonely
Any day, any hour, any moment that she is not around
Pretending …that when I stand behind this mic
That it is she and I and no one else is around….

My Medley of a Great Platter

Now this is the first time that I have ever done this piece
So believe me when I say that this was written for "Only
You (and you alone)" much like the previous poem that was
inspired by The Great Pretender...I showed up tonight and
asked for the manager only to find out that "Maggie Doesn't
Work Here Anymore" you see she had the greatest smile on
this side of the Mississippi...I called it "Heaven on Earth"
but if you never met her "You'll Never, Never Know"
Now I can go on and on about a pretty lady...but soon
"Twilight Time" will be upon us so I will complete this soon
praying that I don't find out "It's Raining Outside"...but if
so I will tell you to follow the Red Sails in the Sunset to the
Harbor Lights and I promise you will make it safely as long
as you don't let The Smoke Get in your eyes...
And remember this great night ...look your love one in the
eyes and tell them tonight that If I didn't care ...I wouldn't
remind you how I love you 1000 times... and if they ask why
tell them
...because you got that magic touch...

Found

Just like roses on a warm spring day
We open to hear what the Heavens have to say
The scriptures tell me that I have found
A good thing
So, you are the song I will forever sing

A Dream, A Dance, A Life

My Dreams become the dance floor
In them we dance the Bachata, Salsa, and
a slow grind…
I wake to see you
It makes my heart dance as swing out,
It dances the tango, the etighi and shoki
You bring Love into my life
You encourage dance into my life
Now we have what many
Hopeless romantics dream about
I just call it Dance…
So, come make Dance to me…

Speechless

For in the Beginning my Heavens shall
Be full of you
In the beginning was
The word and the word was
So good
I wanted to taste you
Echoes of the first days
Say…let there be
Yet…
I Am
Speechless...

The Way I Talk

I want my writings to cause you to be speechless for at least two minutes...
Not because you have nothing to say, but because your emotions have been stirred so well that your questions can't come out of your mouth as fast as they were formed...
your excitement is as fresh as newborn...
inspiration can't be fully enjoyed if you don't allow the first wave of enlightenment to engulf you...call me your Typhoon...the force of my current will come to shore real soon...my tide can't be clocked so no dawn, dusk or high noon, ...I will try to be gentle but my mental will break your levee...my tongue vibes are heavy...my you find vowels forming bodies of expressions with my vocabulary

Dance For Two

Two souls
ready to disco
so, my dreams
become the dance floor
and in them we dance
the Bachata, Salsa
and a little slow grind
...I wake to see you
and it makes my heart dance a swing out,
the Tango, the Etighi and Shoki ...
you bring love into my life
so, with every two steps
...I just call it dance

Ty Foard

Soul Kiss

She had a dream of me kissing her lips...
I woke up wanting to kiss her soul...

Sweet Dreams

I was watching as you fell asleep.
You were sleeping so lovely after counting sheep
And you never once noticed that it was me sitting next to
Little Bo Peep
…I left her with her sheep
Cause I was more interested in
Watching you in your sleep…
…you were holding on to a star
And when I tried to touch you, but your heart seemed to be
so far
So I grabbed hold to a comet
Just to get to where you were…
The universe became our dating place
With no one else in sight I mean not even a trace
Each star was ours
And our bed was on the Red planet of Mars
Saturn rings were our dance floor
And Jupiter Uranus, and Neptune was ours to explore
With Pluto at the back and Mercury covering the front doors.
Venus couldn't stay because she was only getting in the
way…

Ty Foard

A sweet dream…where two became a team…
So, when you win I win …and when I win you win…

You Made Good

...broken and heavy hearted I came to you
...darkened paths and skies dark blue
...just a quick look and you knew just what to do
while other women have no earthly clue...
as the rivers of doubt began to rise in my mind,
you took and held your hand in mine-
with sensations of your touch moving to my heart
I felt like a child all over again...
...see you made good to me
good to me...
intimately...emotionally and we thank God it got
spiritually...good to me...
so, sanctify and purify me by touching me when I was heavy
knowing this world don't understand why I made you my
queen
...well...that's because you made good to me
then I watched as your lips began to part
noticing that they were wet...I mean they were aiming at my
heart
flowing with words to build me-
and fill me-

lovely words that un-killed me-
and the more you spoke the bigger I got-
and the bigger I am the more we will rock…
as our ears listen to the time tic-toc away
this was supposed to be the closing of the day…
and now you've got me excited
and I'm set to make your body my prey…
as we began to lay-
on the bed of true love moments and hours away…
from the start of many climaxes to come-
so are you ready…ready to come…with me…wait on me
same time…let's make sure we do this in rhyme
I'm ready and it's all because of you, you see
Cause baby you made good to me…good to me…
spiritually…intimately…physically…
Really…deeply…smoothly…
you made good to me

My Heaven

We can be one in heavenly matrimony...and I vow to only
explore your planetary mass...bless me
Making love to you shall be my ministry
as we lay on the hot beds of Mercury...with my hands sliding
up your smooth legs as you prepare me to be consume by
your Venus cloud traps...and cover me with your mother
nature like Earth gaps...
laying down face to face or even lap in lap
having me reach for the red peaks of Mars wishing on
romantic stars with all the size of Jupiter
as we go for rounds and rounds on the icy rings of Saturn...
you see to explore our cosmos will show how deep love can
go
as time slips from 7 moons to every noon's
and in our universe the only sin is me not able to hold on to
you...reminding you every day that I love you...
through the fire the only hell will be living outside of you...
so, my faith will be mounted like wings
as I angel my way to you...
above cloud 9's to elevens...
God has allowed you to be my Heaven.

My Heaven 2

So, in my wildest dreams god gave me a wish...
and with that I wanted to create my own universe
and its strings would hang from the fabrics of my poetry's
every verse...
trapped by your eyes my heart wants to burst with your love's
curse...
and my army would be winging legions of angels...
and on these clouds, I create my own epiphanies...
And my Genesis will Exodus us...and in the beginning there
is me...and before me I speak let there be... Creation started
with a wine hypnotic like verse
So metaphoric so exotic...that it will be Bibled into a poetic
epic...always being listed in the table of contents of any
lover's topic...served in wine flutes...to play for the lovers of
love as they take lips to drink it...
Cool cats sit back in semi black spoken word nights thinking
about it...
Neo soiling about it...leaving in the middle of mid-nights to
talk about it...
Till morning dawns set in your south...I will east all of you

till you are so west we shake to the north of stars and our
midnights become seven...I created a position and place for
you and called you my Heaven
The gem of my creation...my life's salvation...
Holy father it's been two days since my last confession, but
she is the destination of all my fixations and admirations...
and thoughts of walking down your golden street to reach
your pearly gates is the source of my erotic stimulation...
to give birth to my Adam...
and in gardens I stand till Eden all of you consume every cell
of me...
and my DNA will make an old and new testament way...
exploding every Adam until the day passes to Eve...
no longer forbidden you are my fruit and holding you close to
me has become my religion...
allowing me to stand up in a romantic...
eclectic fashion...I long to lay in your many mansions
blowing my horn of Gabriel as you bless me by beating on
my drums and on vended knees...
our seeds pray for our kingdom to come...and thy will be
done...as we speak with vibrate tongues...were a lifetime of
love turns into eternity...

Fall... Grow... Dream... Build

I want to fall in love
with you every day
everyday as if it was the first day
hold on to you like it's the last day
and dream with you as if we have forever
and a day...
If tomorrow ever comes... will you come
back?
So, I can love you all over again
But maybe better than before...
I want to grow in love with you today
and tomorrow that growth will bloom
And the next day will be our harvest...
I want to ... fall ... grow... dream ...build...
love

I See Your Eyes

What are you saying when you look at me
like that
I see your eyes... and I can't interpret
their vision talk
...like you lips are sealed... but I need to
know their secret...
I need to know their desires, their
destinations...
Are they talking about us... are they
speaking to the Lord?
Are they blessing us... no bended knee
needed...Amen...?
Be the Savior to my curiosity...
What are you saying when you look at me
like that...
I see your eyes

Go Left And Stop Looking Right

Erotic
You wanted it tonight
But I want you in plain sight
And maybe we both just got so turned
On that we got wet before
A single drop of rain ever hit us right…
Stop it before it starts to slide
Down your leg
No panties…
They were left off tonight
So, our rendezvous was a spot in the rain
Between your valley and these lines
I wrote this…
But together we can take advantage of
much needed bliss…
I like what you like
So, my sensuality licked that spot that liked
We did this like
An unbothered Adam and Eve

Cause no man, woman, or god
Is our boss…
So, there are no commandment or lines to cross
Just our boldness to please each other
Throughout the passions of this night…
This love gives us new sight
Out of Eden
I hang to the left of things
So, don't go looking right.

Online

erotic

Every hour I check to see if you are online
In hopes that I can send
An instant message of
Love rhymes
Downloaded into the inline regions of your heart
And that will be where our internet fantasies start
Through your blog post
I can hear the increase of your breathing
Sweet but silent blow…
Every keystroke set off
chain reactions of affections
like orgasmic injections
hard on like erections
until you receive every upload
of this hyperlink
I await feeling the high-speed connection
Of your keystrokes…
light screams make the sweetest high notes
It is those high notes that

Eros: Psalms of Love

Let's me know that you
Received every picture note
Emailed to you across this vast internet highway
We play tag
In a playful karma sutra position kind of way
Making the www
Fit our favorite way
Took Myspace off the page
Cause you preferred my Facebook into your space
Bigger than Blackplanet
Pink laced Vicky can't keep secrets
So, we got the shivers no need to twitter…
Got DM'd them moment you accepted my Linkin
My body is on edge when you
Played my full house card…seeing you sign on
Got me logging on hard.

Ty Foard

About Ty Foard

Ty, has writing poetry and short stories since a child. Once becoming a musical theater and drama student, his interest in writing in those areas increased. As of date he has written over fifteen stage plays and has produced eight of them. Ty also has been the host of an award winning online radio show title "Ty & The Sips" since 2010. In 2015, he launch I AM Royalty Radio, a 24/7 internet radio station. As an accomplished Poet/Spoken Word artist he has performed on many stages around the country. His unique way of engaging his audience with his Poetic Wine brand of poetry, has landed him several awards and accomplishments. In early 2011, he was diagnose with stage 4 Hodgkin's Lymphoma. During his battle with the cancer he found himself bedridden and writing was the only thing that the battle hadn't stopped him from doing at ease. His bout with cancer was the inspiration to publish some of his work for his desire is to share love, hope and inspiration to others.

Eros: Psalms of Love